Sentient Beings in the Kingdom of Bhutan

Laurie S. Chambers

Balboa Press books may be ordered through booksellers or by contacting:

Balboa Press
A Division of Hay House
1663 Liberty Drive
Bloomington, IN 47403
www.balboapress.com
1 (877) 407-4847

Photographs by Laurie S. Chambers

Artwork by Cindy A. Chambers and Breanna Chambers

ISBN: 978-1-9822-3270-2 (sc)
ISBN: 978-1-9822-3271-9 (e)

Library of Congress Control Number: 2019911473

Print information available on the last page.

Balboa Press rev. date: 08/20/2019

BALBOA.
PRESS
A DIVISION OF HAY HOUSE

Nowhere in the world will you feel a more overwhelming sense of something greater than yourself than in the Kingdom of Bhutan. It is a feeling evoked not only by the mysterious beauty that is inescapable as far as the eyes can see, but also from the vibrations that are held by those who live and breathe there and know what it is to be a sentient being and continue to strive in the light and teachings of the Buddha.

The tiny and remote Kingdom of Bhutan is nestled in the Himalayas between China and India. The mostly Buddhist populace is so strong in its belief that a sentient being should be cared for and not harmed that the killing of animals and fish is not allowed in Bhutan. A person could be arrested and fined for it. This also applies to accidentally killing a stray dog. Consequently, stray dogs have a place in the community and live in harmony with humans.

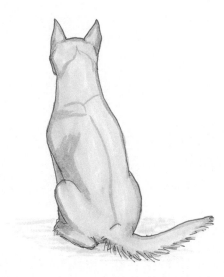

Canadian barrister Lloyd Duhaime's Law
Dictionary defines a sentient being as

"a creature that can suffer and feel
pain, mostly animals and humans."

<http://www.duhaime.org/LegalDictionary/S/SentientBeing.aspx />

The Buddha expounded that sentient beings currently living in the animal realm have been our mothers, brothers, sisters, fathers, children, and friends in past incarnations. Ultimately, humans and animals are part of a single family. We are all interconnected.

Sentient beings have an awareness of themselves and the ability to sense or feel things and show responsiveness. It is so very extraordinary that we can experience through our senses all the emotions and feelings that make us special—not just those of pain and suffering, but also of happiness…

Loyalty...

Attachment…

Contentment…

Attentiveness …

Mindfulness…

Trust…

Curiosity…

Love

Something in your eyes
Took a thousand years to get here
Something in your eyes
Took a thousand years, a thousand years

Hold me close
Hold me close and don't let me go
Hold me close
Like I'm someone that you might know

U2, Songs of Innocence. "Iris (Hold Me Close)." Adam Clayton/Dave

Evans/Larry Mullen Jr/Paul David Hewson. September, 2014.

According to the Mahayana Buddhist
school of thought, all animals,
including dogs, have always been
regarded as sentient beings.

They possess Buddha nature, and therefore
have the potential for enlightenment.

The creatures that inhabit
this earth—be they human
beings or animal—are here
to contribute, each in its own
particular way, to the beauty
and prosperity of the world.

—The Fourteenth Dalai Lama

There is a sense of community and loyalty among the dogs in Bhutan. Psychologists McMillan and Chavis define a sense of community as "a feeling that members have of belonging, a feeling that members matter to one another and to the group, and a shared faith that members' needs will be met through their commitment to be together."

McMillan, D. W. & Chavis, D. M. (1986). Sense of community: A definition and theory. *Journal of Community Psychology*, 14(1), 6-23.

People in Bhutan think or believe dogs are their ancestors; in general Buddhist believe dogs are also sentient beings and they need to be cared for and not harmed … let them live. Buddhist believe that if you take a sentient being's life, you are preventing that being from living out its Karma in its present form.

—Namgay Dorgi, Founder and CEO,

Step 2 Bhutan Tours and Treks

Whenever I trek in Bhutan, I am always accompanied by many of these four-legged shepherds. It's a comforting feeling while exploring in "their" cities and mountains, as though they are looking after me. The dogs are like visual, spiritual, protective anchors to and of the past, a constant reminder of the heritage and culture of Bhutan. Kind of like New Age gargoyles … always behind the scenes, ever vigilant, keeping the spiritual/mystical plane in balance. Four-legged talismans, conduits (I think) between the physical planes of the past and present. These old souls always make me smile.

—Martin McGinnis, friend and fellow trekker

Come to
teach, come
to be taught,
come in the
likeness in the
image of God,
cause you can
be like that,
with all that
humbleness
and all that
respect.

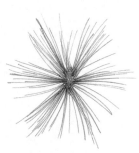

Nahko Bear and Medicine for the

People - "Aloha *Ke Akua*." 2013.

Whatever our roles
or purposes,

As we move
through the seasons
of our lives,

Every step of the way,

We are all
looked after.

At every turn or
open door, as
we are about to
move forward,

We are assisted,

Encouraged,

And helped.

Shepherded, if you will;

Guided by an unseen force
along the path we chose before
drawing our first breaths.

LOVE

Unconditional and beyond
all human comprehension.

And in life known by humans, sentient beings of the highest order … we will inevitably find ourselves in situations that feel as if we are on the edge.

Knowing there is a greater hand ever-present to lift us up

And carry us on… is priceless.

We are all sentient beings, gifted with purpose and ability to uplift human spirit! So as you walk about this amazing planet we call Earth, strive to do your best in thought, word, and deed. Do it with love, in the manner of the four-legged ones, without hesitation or expectation. Raise the vibration around you, and feel the abundance of love and joy already present, just waiting for you to accept.

With grace and blessings of the love and the light,

In the mid-2000s, the "community of dogs," while serving a purpose and an important part of Bhutan's ecosystem, was getting a little out of hand. The Bhutanese government reached out to Humane Society International (H.S.I.) for help. H.S.I. suggested that Bhutan initiate a nationwide spay-neuter-vaccination program, where the dogs are humanely captured with nets, treated, and released the same day in the same location they were found. With the help of H.S.I. and support by the government, a complete program was launched that included the training of a Bhutanese team of veterinarians, vet techs, and dog catchers trained in special techniques. Door-to-door mass education for the public, including the monks, emphasized the importance of health care for all dogs. Programs were established to enable people to bring in their dogs for free vaccinations and sterilizations that also served to promote and enhance responsible pet ownership.

Bhutan has become the premier model for the humane management of large dog populations that have a life of living wild and free with this method. As of 2018, nine years after the inception of H.S.I.'s program, approximately 85,000 of the original estimated 100,000 dogs living in the country have undergone sterilization and vaccinations, stabilizing the population. Over time, the number of dogs will naturally decline, but there will always be a significant community of dogs. Anyone who visits Bhutan will easily see that both dogs and people, sentient beings all, live in a harmonious relationship, supporting each other's needs.

About the Author

Free-spirited with a gypsy soul, Laurie Chambers has spent
over 50 years traveling the planet, searching for the heart of
each community she can explore. While seeking to understand
the complexity of being human, she's captured a global array
of cultures, customs, and the traditions of indigenous people
that create the uniqueness of every place on this Earth.

Her mission: to inspire and uplift all beings along her
path, believing that all souls serve equal purpose and
knowing that great love is always just a moment away.

Printed in the United States
By Bookmasters